I0136475

Anonymous

A Vocabulary of Technical Terms Used in Elementary

Vernacular School Books

Hindustani-English

Anonymous

A Vocabulary of Technical Terms Used in Elementary Vernacular School Books
Hindustani-English

ISBN/EAN: 9783744644785

Printed in Europe, USA, Canada, Australia, Japan

Cover: Foto ©Andreas Hilbeck / pixelio.de

More available books at **www.hansebooks.com**

A VOCABULARY

OF

TECHNICAL TERMS

USED IN

ELEMENTARY VERNACULAR SCHOOL BOOKS,

HINDUSTANI-ENGLISH.

For the use of European Educational Officers in the Punjab preparing for the Departmental Examination in Hindustani.

ISSUED TO THE

EDUCATIONAL DEPARTMENT PUNJAB,

BY ORDER OF

DR. G. W. LEITNER,

Officiating Director of Public Instruction, Punjab.

LAHORE :

GOVERNMENT CENTRAL BOOK DEPOT.

1879.

1st Edition : 200 Copies.

Price 12 Annas.

Circular.

The first edition of the Vocabulary of Technical Terms used in elementary Vernacular School books is herewith circulated with the request of the officiating Director of Public Instruction, Punjab, that the officers of the Department may kindly suggest additions or corrections for a second enlarged and revised edition.

VOCABULARY of HINDUSTÁNÍ TECHNICAL TERMS used in the Vernacular School-books of the Punjab.

Vocabulary of Hindustání Technical Terms used in Vernacular School books of the Punjab

Hindustání Technical Terms used in ordinary Vernacular Educational books.		Their Equivalents or Meanings in English.
A.		
Ábná	اُبنا	A strait, (Geography).
'Adad	عدد	Number, (Arithmetic).
'Adad-i-Mafrúz	عددِفرض	A given number, (Do.)
'Ádd	عاد	A measure ; a factor, (Do.)
'Ádd-i-A'zam	عادِاعظم	The greatest common measure, (Arithmetic and Algebra).
'Ádd-i-Mushtarik	عادِمشترک	A common measure, (Do.)
A'dád-i-Muta'alliq	اعدادِمتعلق	Concrete numbers, (Do.)
A'dád-i-Mutabain	اعدادِمتباین	Prime numbers (Do.)
A'dád-i-Mutanásib 'ala-t-tawálí	اعدادِمتناسب علی التوالی	Numbers in continued Proportion, (Algebra)
A'dád-i-Mutawásiq	اعدادِمتوافق	Composite numbers, (Arithmetic).
A'dád-i-Mutawátir	اعدادِمتواتر	The Periods or Repetends in circulating Decimals, (Do.)
A'dád-i-Mutlaq	اعدادِمطلق	Abstract numbers, (Do.)
'Adad-i-Sahíh	عددِصحیح	A whole number or integer, (Do.)
'Adad-i-Sar	عددِسر	A co-efficient, (Algebra).
Af'áli-Náqisa	افعالِناقصہ	See Fi'l-i-Náqis, (Grammar).
Af'áli-Qulúb	افعالِقلوب	Verbs signifying actions that take place in the mind, as thinking, believing, knowing, &c., (Grammar)

Ajrám-i-Falakí	اجرامِ فلکی	Heavenly bodies, sun, moon, stars, planets &c., (Geography)
Ajzá	اجزا	Parts, (Algebra).
Ajzá-i-Gair-Mutanásila	اجزائے غیر متناسلہ	Unlike quantities or terms, (Do.)
Ajzá-i-Jundn-i-Jabríyu	اجزائے جدرِ جبریہ	The terms of an Algebraical expression, (Do.)
Ajzá-i-Mutamásila	اجزائے متماثلہ	Like quantities or terms, (Do.)
Ajzá-i-Muttahid-ul-quwá	اجزائے متحدالقوی	Terms of like powers or dimensions, (Do.)
Ajzá-i-Zarbí	اجزائے ضربی	Factors, (Do.)
'Alámat-i-Juzí	علامتِ جزری	The Radical sign, (Do.)
'Alámat-i-Nafy, yá 'Alámat-i-Farq	علامتِ نفی ۔ یا علامتِ فرق	The sign minus, (Do.)
'Alámat-i-Isbát yá 'Alámat-i-Jamá'	علامتِ اثبات ۔ یا علامتِ جمع	The sign plus, (Do.)
'Alámat-i-Musáwát	علامتِ مساوات	The sign equal, (Do.)
'Alámat-i-Nuzúlí	علامتِ نزولی	The Radical sign, (Do.)
'Alámat-i-Tankír	علامتِ تنکیر	The sign of an indeterminate noun, as "koi," "kuchh," (Grammar).
'Alam	علم	(1) a Gnomon, (Euclid); (2) a proper noun, (Grammar).
Alif-l-Mamdúda	الف ممدودہ	A prolonged alif marked with the sign madd آ (Do.)
Alif-i-Maqsúra	الف مقصورہ	A short alif frequently taking the form of (ی) Ye, as اعلیٰ A'lá, (Grammar).
'Amal	عمل	Process, (Arithmetic).
'Amal-i-Zihní	عملِ ذہنی	Mental process, (Do.)
'Amúd	عمود	A Perpendicular, (Euclid)
Árat	आरत	A commission received on sale of goods, (Arithmetic).

Vocabulary of Hindustáni Technical Terms.—continued.

HINDUSTÁNÍ TECHNICAL TERMS used in ordinary VERNACULAR EDUCATIONAL BOOKS.		THEIR EQUIVALENTS OR MEANINGS IN ENGLISH.
A.		
Arba'a-i-Mutanásiba	اربعۀ متناسبه	The Single Rule of Three, (Arithmetic).
Arba'a-i-Mutanásiba-i-Rást	اربعۀ متناسبۀ راست	The Direct Rule of Three, (Do.)
Arba'a-i-Mutanásiba-i-Ma'kús	اربعۀ متناسبۀ معکوس	The Inverse Rule of Three, (Do.)
Arkán-i-Jumla	ارکان جمله	The terms of an Algebraical expression, (Algebra).
'Arz	عرض	Breadth, (Arithmetic).
'Arz-i-Balad	عرض بلد	Latitude, (Geography).
Ashkál-i-Mujessama	اشکال مجسمه	Solid figures, (Euclid).
Ashkál-i-Mustaqímat-ul-Azlá'	اشکال مستقیمة الاضلاع	} Rectilineal figures, (Do.)
Ashkál-i-Mustaqímat-ul-Khutút	اشکال مستقیمة الخطوط	
'Atf-ba-Harf	عطف بحرف	A connection of nouns or sentences by a conjunction, (Grammar).
'Atfi-Bayán	عطف بیان	An explanatory Apposition, as *Sa'dí* in *Muslíh-ud-dín Sa'dí*, (Grammar).
Atráf	اطراف	The extreme terms of a proportion, (Algebra).
Atráf-i-Musáwát	اطراف مساوات	} The sides of an equation, (Algebra).
Arkán-i-Musáwát	ارکان مساوات	
Ausát	اوساط	The mean terms of a proportion (Do.)
Az'áf	اضعاف	Multiples, (Arithmetic, Algebra, Euclid).

اضلاعِ نظیر	The Homologous sides (Do.)
بدل	A substitute ; a noun in apposition, as *Tumhárí bháí*, in, *Zaid tumhárí bháí áyá* (Grammar).
بدر	The full moon, (Geography).
بحر	An ocean, (Do.)
بحرالجزائر	An Archipelago, (Do.)
باقی	Remainder, (Arithmetic)
براعظم	A continent, ((Geography).
بیابان	A desert, (Do.)
بحیرہ	A sea, (Do.)
बीमा	Insurance, (Arithmetic)
دہائی	The tens, (Arithmetic).
بہاو	The mouth of a river. (Geography).
دائرہ	A circle, (Euclid).
दक्खन	The South, (Geography).
دلالی	Brokerage, (Arithmetic).
دقیقہ	A minute, (Arithmetic).
درجہ	A degree, (Do.)

Vocabulary of Hindustání Technical Terms.—continued.

HINDUSTÁNÍ TECHNICAL TERMS USED IN ORDINARY VERNACULAR EDUCATIONAL BOOKS.		THEIR EQUIVALENTS OR MEANINGS IN ENGLISH
D.		
Daryá...........	دریا	A river, (Geography).
Dostúrí........	دستوری	A perquisite paid to servants by merchants who sell any goods to their masters, (Arithmetic).
Dawáir-i Mutanássa....	دوائرِ متناسبه	Circles that touch one another, (Euclid).
Dawáir-i Mutasáwiya....	دوائرِ متساویہ	Equal circles, (Do.)
Dawáir-i Qutbi	دوائرِ قطبی	The Polar circles, (Geography).
Dum-dár Saiyára	دم دار سیارہ	A comet, (Do.)
F.		
Fá'il................	فاعل	An agent. The Nominative case, (Grammar).
Farq-i-'Ámm........	فرقِ عام	The common difference, (Arithmetic).
Fásil-i-Áb...........	فاصلِ آب	A watershed, (Geography).
Fasl-i-Mushtarik	فصلِ مشترک	The common section, (Euclid).
Fi'l................	فعل	A Verb, (Grammar).
Fi'l-i-Amr............	فعلِ امر	An affirmative Imperative Verb, (Grammar).
Fi'l-i-Amr-i-Mudámi....	فعلِ امرِ مدامی	Do. Do. implying continuity as "Parhte-raho," (Do.)
Fi'l-i-Hál............	فعلِ حال	The Present Imperfect, (Do.)
Fi'l-i-Lázim........	فعلِ لازم	An Intransitive Verb, (Do.)

Fi'l-i-Lázim-i-Maḥdúd	خبر ذارکردہ	An Intransitive Verb which will not admit a Transitive form, (Grammar).
Fi'l-i-Majhúl	خبرمجہول	The Passive Voice, (Do.)
Fi'l-i-Manfi	خبرمنفی	A Negative Verb, (Do.)
Fi'l-i-Ma'rúf	خبرمعروف	The Active Voice, (Do.)
Fi'l-i-Mází	خبرماضی	The Preterite, (Do.)
Fi'l-i-Mázi-i-Ba'íd	خبرماضی بعید	The Past Perfect, (Do.)
Fi'l-i-Mázi-i-Ihtimálí	خبرماضی احتمالی	The Future Perfect, or Past Potential, (Do.)
Fi'l-i-Mázi-i-Istimrárí	خبرماضی استمراری	The Past Continuous, (Do.)
Fi'l-i-Mázi-i-Ma'túf	خبرماضی معطوف	The Past Conjunctive Participle as " *Parh-kar chalí gayí*," (Do.)
Fi'l-i-Mázi-i-Mutlaq	خبرماضی مطلق	The Past Indefinite, (Do.)
Fi'l-i-Mázi-ná-tamám	خبرماضی ناتمام	The Past Continuous, (Do.)
Fi'l-i-Mázi-i-Qaríb	خبرماضی قریب	The Present Perfect, (Do.)
Fi'l-i-Mázi-i-Shakkí	خبرماضی شکی	The Future Perfect or Past Potential, (Do.)
Fi'l-i-Mázi-i-Shartí	خبرماضی شرطی	The Past Optative or Conditional, (Do.)
Fi'l-i-Mází-i-Tamanná-í	خبرماضی تمنائی	
Fi'l-i-Musbat	خبرمثبت	An Affirmative Verb, (Do.)
Fi'l-i-Mustaqbil	خبرمستقبل	The Future tense, (Do.)
Fi'l-i-Muta'addí	خبرمتعدی	The Transitive Verb, (Do.)
Fi'l-i-Muta'addí-ba-yak-Maf'úl	خبرمتعدی بیک مفعول	A Transitive Verb having only one object, (Do.)
Fi'l-i-Muta'addí-ba-do-Maf'úl	خبرمتعدی بدو مفعول	Do. having 2 objects, (Do.)

Vocabulary of Hindustání Technical Terms.—continued.

HINDUSTÁNÍ TECHNICAL TERMS used in ordinary VERNACULAR EDUCATIONAL BOOKS.		THEIR EQUIVALENTS OR MEANINGS IN ENGLISH.
F.		
Fi'l-i-Muta'addi ba sih Maf'úl	خاص متعدی به سه مفعول	A Transitive verb having 3 objects, (Grammar).
Fi'l-i-Muta'addi bi-l-wásita	متعدی بالواسطه	A Causal Verb, (Do.)
Fi'l-i-Muta'addi bi-Nafsi-hí	متعدی بنفسه	A Verb which is Transitive per se, (Do.)
Fi'l-i-Muta'addi-i-Mahdúd	متعدی محدود	A Transitive Verb which will not admit the Causative form, (Do.)
Fi'l-i-Muta'addi-ul-Muta'addi	متعدی المتعدی	A doubly Transitive or doubly Causative Verb, as *Parháná*, (Do.)
Fi'l-i-Muzári'	مضارع	The Aorist, (Do.)
Fi'l-i-Nahy	نهی	The Negative Imperative Mood of a Verb, (Do.)
Fi'l-i-Náqis	ناقص	An incomplete Verb, (Do.)
Fi'l-i-Qalb	قلب	See Afál-i-qulúb, (Do.)
Fi'l-i-Támm	تام	A complete Verb, (Do.)
Fi-Sadi	فی صدی	Per cent, (Arithmetic).
G		
Gahn	गहन	An Eclipse, (Geography).
Gáib	غائب	The person spoken of, or the 3rd person, (Grammar).
Gair-Musáwí	غیر مساوی	Unequal, (Euclid).
Gair-Mushtaqq	غیر مشتق	A primitive word, (Grammar).

Gair-Zawi-i-'Uqúl	غيرذوى العقل	Irrational, (Grammar)
Gardán	گردان	Conjugation, Declension, (Do.)
Gardish-i-Zamín	گردش زمين	The motion or revolution of the Earth, (Geography).
Gardish-i-Mihwarí	گردش محورى	The Earth's revolution on its axis, (Do.)
Ghátí	گھاٹى	A Valley, (Do.)
Ginti	گنتى	Number, (Arithmetic).
Gosha-i-Janúb-o-Magrib	گوشه جنوب و مغرب	The South-West corner, (Geography).
Gosha-i-Janúb-o-Mashriq	گوشه جنوب و مشرق	The South-East corner. (Do.)
Gosha-i-Shamál-o-Magrib	گوشه شمال و مغرب	The North-West corner, (Do.)
Gosha-i-Shamál-o-Mashriq	گوشه شمال و مشرق	The North-East corner, (Do.)
Guzar-gáh-i-Daryá	گزرگاه دريا	The bed of a river, (Do.)
H		
Há-i-Mukhtafí	ہاے مختفى	The mute he (ہ) as in *Parwána* (پروانہ), (Grammar).
Hadd	حد	The term or boundary, (Euclid).
Hál	حال	A word shewing the circumstance or state of a nominative or objective, (Gram.).
Hall	حل	A solution, (Arithmetic and Algebra).
Ham-Irtifá'	ہم ارتفاع	Having the same altitude, (Euclid).
Handasa	ہندسہ	A Numerical figure, (Arithmetic).
Harakat-i-Rozána	حركت روزانہ	The diurnal motion of the Earth, (Geography).
Harakat-i-Sáálana	حركت سالانہ	The annual revolution of the Earth, (Do.)

H.

....

-i-Bayán .... A Particle, (Grammar).

-i-'Illat .... An Explicative Particle, (Do.)

-i-'Illat .... A long Vowel— ا (*alif*), و (*wáo*) or ی (*ye*), (Do.)

.... A corollary, (Euclid).

-i-'Amal .... The result of an operation or process, (Arithmetic and Algebra).

-i-Jama' .... The sum or amount of several numbers, (Do.)

-i-Masdar .... A Verbal Noun, (Grammar).

-i-Tafríq .... The difference or remainder, (Arithmetic).

-i-Zarb......... The product, (Do.)

.... Elision, (Grammar).

.... The new Moon, (Geography).

asa. .... See Handasa.

>-i-Mu'áwaza .... Exchange, (Arithmetic).

>-i-Naf-'o-Nuqsán .... Profit and Loss, (Do.)

>-i-Roz-marrah .... } Practice, (Do.)

>-i-Tijárat ....

		Definitions, (Euclid).
Hadúd	عدد	
Hurúf-i-'Atf..........	حروف عطف	Copulative Particles, (Grammar).
Hurúf-i-Íjáb	حروف ایجاب	Particles of affirmation or assent, (Do.)
Hurúf-i-Ikhtisás	حروف اختصاص	Particles of identity or specification, as *hí* in (*wuh tú hí hai*), (Do.)
Hurúf-i-Imbisát	حروف انبساط	Particles of joy and admiration, (Do.)
Hurúf-i-Istidrák	حروف استدراک	Adversative Particles, as *par, lekin*, (Do.)
Hurúf-i-Istisná	حروف استثنا	Exceptive Particles, as *siwá*, (Do.)
Hurúf-i-Izáfat	حروف اضافت	Particles of annexation, as *ká, kí*, (Do.)
Hurúf-i-Jarr	حروف جر	Particles of attraction. Prepositions, (Do.)
Hurúf-i-Járr	حروف جار	
Hurúf-i-Jawáb	حروف جواب	The Particles used in answering questions, (Do.)
Hurúf-i-Jazá	حروف جزا	Particles of consequence, as *to* in (*áp kaheṇ to maiṇ jáúṇ*), (Do.)
Hurúf-i-Miqdár	حروف مقدار	Particles of quantity, (Do.)
Hurúf-i-Mugaiyirah	حروف مغیره	The Particles *meṇ, se, ko, tak,* &c. which, when preceded by the Personal Pronoun of the 3rd Person in the Nominative case, cause it to be changed as *wuh* is changed into *us* when joined to *ko* (*us ko*), (Do.)
Hurúf-i-Nafy	حروف نفی	Particles of Negation, (Do.)
Hurúf-i-Nidá	حروف ندا	The Vocative Particles, (Do).
Hurúf-i-Shart	حروف شرط	Particles of condition, (Do.)
Hurúf-i-Shirkat	حروف شرکت	Particles of Participation, as *bhí* in *wuh bhí maujúd hai*, (Do.)
Hurúf-i-Taassuf	حروف تاسف	Particles of lamentation, (Do.)

Vocabulary of Hindustáni Technical Terms.—continued.

Hindustáni Technical Terms used in ordinary Vernacular Educational Books.		Their Equivalents or Meanings in English.
H.		
Hurúf-i-Tambíh	درونِ تنبیه	Particles of warning, (Grammar).
Hurúf-i-Tardíd	درونِ تردید	Disjunctive Particles, (Do.)
Hurúf-i-Tashbíh	درونِ تشبیه	Particles of similitude as sá in chánd sá chihra, (Do.)
Hurúf-i-Zarfiyat	درونِ ظرفیت	Particles of place or time, (Do.)
I.		
Ikái	اِکائی	A Unit, (Arithmetic).
Ikhtisár	اختصار	The simplification or reduction of an Arithmetical or Algebraical sum,
'Ilm-i-Riyázi	علمِ ریاضی	Mathematics.
Imtihán	امتحان	Proof, (Arithmetic).
Intiqál	انتقال	Transposition, (Algebra).
Irtifá'	ارتفاع	Altitude, (Euclid).
Ism	اسم	A Noun, (Grammar).
Ism-i-'Adad	اسمِ عدد	A Numeral, (Do.)
Ism-i-Ála	اسمِ آلہ	A Noun of instrument, (Do.)
Ism-i-'Alam	اسمِ علم	A Proper Noun, (Do.)
Ism-i-Fá'il	اسمِ فاعل	A Noun of Agency, (Do.)
Ism-i-Háliya	اسمِ حالیہ	An Imperfect Participle. (Do.)

Ism-i-Ishára.........	اسم اشاره	A Demonstrative Pronoun, (Grammar).
Ism-i-Istifhám........	اسم استفهام	An Interrogative Pronoun, (Do).
Ism-i-Jama'.........	اسم جمع	A Collective Noun, (Do).
Ism-i-Jámid.........	اسم جامد	A Primitive Noun, (Do).
Ism-i-Jins	اسم جنس	A Generic Noun, (Do).
Ism-i-Maf'úl	اسم مفعول	The Perfect or Passive Participle, (Do).
Ism-i-Makán	اسم مکان	A noun of place, (Do).
Ism-i-Ma'rifa	اسم معرفه	A Determinate Noun, (Do).
Ism-i-Mausúl	اسم موصول	A Relative Pronoun, (Do).
Ism-i-Mushtaqq	اسم مشتق	A Derivative Noun, (Do).
Ism-i-Nakira	اسم نکره	An Indeterminate Noun, (Do).
Ism-i-Saut	اسم صوت	(A Noun of sound). An Interjectional word used to drive away an animal, or to denote its peculiar noise as káoŋ, káoŋ (the cawing of a crow), (Do).
Ism-i-Sifat	اسم صفت	An Adjective, (Do).
Ism-i-Tafzíl.........	اسم تفضیل	An Adjective of the superlative degree, (Do).
Ism-i-Tasgír	اسم تصغیر	A Diminutive Noun, (Do).
Ism-i-Zamán	اسم زمان	A Noun of time, (Do).
Ism-i-Zarf	اسم ظرف	A Noun of time or place, (Do).
Ism-i-Zamír.........	اسم ضمیر	A Personal Pronoun, (Do).
Ism-i-Zát.........	اسم ذات	A Noun Substantive, (Do).

HINDUSTÁNÍ TECHNICAL TERMS USED IN ORDINARY VERNACULAR EDUCATIONAL BOOKS.		THEIR EQUIVALENTS OR MEANINGS IN ENGLISH.
I.		
Isnád	اسناد	The relation that subsists between a subject and its Predicate, (Grammar).
Istiʿára...............	استعارہ	A metaphor, (Do).
Istifhám-i-'Adadí	استفہام عددی	A Numeral Interrogative, as *kaí* (how many ?), (Do).
Istifhám-i-Miqdárí	استفہام مقداری	An Interrogative of quantity, as *kitná* (how much ?), (Do.)
Istifhám-i-Sababí	استفہام سببی	An Interrogation of cause, as *kyon* (why ?), (Do).
Istigráq	استغراق	The comprehensive form of a Numeral Adjective, as *cháron shakhs*, meaning *all the four persons*, (Grammar).
Izáfat-i-Lafzí	اضافت لفظی	Verbal annexation, (Do).
Izáfat-i-Maʿnawí	اضافت معنوی	Logical Do. (Do.)
Izáfat-i-Takhsísí	اضافت تخصیصی	An *Izáfat* which peculiarizes the governing noun to its genitive, as *Ghoṛé-kí-káṭhí* (Grammar).
Izáfat-i-Tauzíhí	اضافت توضیحی	An *Izáfat* whereby the genitive explains its governing noun, as *Anár-ká darakht*, (Grammar).
J.		
Jabr-o-Muqábala....	جبر و مقابلہ	Algebra.
Jamaʿ	جمع	1. Plural, (Grammar); 2 Addition, (Arithmetic).
Jamʿ-i-Murakkab	جمع مرکب	Compound addition, (Do).
Jamʿ-ul-Jamaʿ'......	جمع الجمع	The Plural of a plural noun, as *Kawágizát*, the plural of *Kawágíz*, the plural of *Káġiz*, (Grammar).

Jangal	جنگل	A forest, (Geography).
Janúb	جنوب	The South, (Do.)
Jawáb	جواب	An answer, (Arithmetic and Algebra).
Jazá	جزا	An apodosis, (Grammar).
Jazr	جذر	The square root of any number, (Arithmetic).
Jazíra	جزیرہ	An Island, (Geography).
Jazíra-Numá	جزیرہ نما	A Peninsula, (Do.)
Jhíl	झील	A Lake, (Do.)
Jism	جسم	A solid body, (Euclid).
Juálá Mukhí Pahár	ज्वालामुखी पहाड़	A Volcano, (Geography).
Juft	جفت	An even number, (Arithmetic).
Jugráfiya	جغرافیہ	Geography.
Jumla	جملہ	A clause or a sentence, (Grammar).
Jumla-i-Bayániya	جملہ بیانیہ	The explicative phrase or clause in a sentence, as *Ma'lúm húá ki tum ek tálib-i-'ilm ho*, (Do).
Jumla-i-Fi'liya	جملہ فعلیہ	A verbal sentence, as *Zaid ne márá* (Do).
Jumla-i-Insháíya	جملہ انشائیہ	A sentence which contains a command or a wish, (Do.)
Jumla-i-Ismíya	جملہ اسمیہ	A nominal sentence, as *zaid ek 'álim hai*, (Do.)
Jumla-i-Jabriya	جملہ جبریہ	An Algebraical expression, (Algebra).
Jumla-i-Jawáb-i-Nidá	جملہ جواب ندا	A clause following a noun in the vocative case to explain the object of invocation, (Grammar).

Vocabulary of Hindustání Technical Terms.—continued.

Hindustání Technical Terms used in ordinary Vernacular Educational Books.		Their Equivalents or Meanings in English.
J.		
Jumla-i-Jawáb-i-Qasam...............	جملۂ جواب قسم	A clause following a word of oath to explain the object of the oath taken (Grammar).
Jumla-i-Jazá	جملۂ جزا	See Jazá, (Grammar).
Jumla-i-kasír-ul-ujzá	جملۂ کثیر الاجزا	A Multinomial expression, (Algebra).
Jumla-i-kasír-ul-arkán	جملۂ کثیر الارکان	
Jumla-i-khabariya	جملۂ خبریہ	An affirmative sentence, as zaid parhtá hai, (Grammar).
Jumla-i-mufrada............	جملۂ مفردہ	A simple Algebraical expression, (Algebra).
Jumla-i-Murakkaba	جملۂ مرکبہ	A compound Algebraical expression, (Do.)
Jumla-i-Mu'tariza	جملۂ معترضہ	A parenthetical clause, (Grammar).
Jumla-i-Nidáiya............	جملۂ ندائیہ	A vocative sentence, (Do.)
Jumla-i-Qasamiya	جملۂ قسمیہ	A sentence which contains an oath, (Do.)
Jumla-i-Sanái............	جملۂ ثنائی	A Binomial, (Algebra).
Jumla-i-Shart............	جملۂ شرط	A protosis, (Grammar).
Jumla-i-Shartíya............	جملۂ شرطیہ	A conditional sentence, (Do.)
Jumla-i-Sulási	جملۂ ثلاثی	A Trinomial, (Algebra).
Jumla-i-Ukhrá	جملۂ اخریٰ	The right side of an Equation, (Algebra).
Jumla-i-Úlá............	جملۂ اولیٰ	The left side Do. (Do.)

Juz	ٔجز	(1) a part, (Euclid). (2) the square root, (Arithmetic).
Juz-ul-ka'b	جزالكعب	The cube root, (Do.)
Juz-ul-Mál	جزالمال	The square root, (Do.)
Juz-i-Mál-ul-Ka'b	جزمال الكعب	The fifth root, (Do.)
Juz-i-Mál-ul-Mál	جزمال المال	The fourth root, (Do.)
Juz-i-Zarbí	جزضربى	A factor, (Do.)

K

Ka'b	كعب	The cube of a quantity, (Do.)
Kalám	كلام	A complete proposition or sentence, (Grammar).
Kalima	كلمه	A word, (Do.)
Kalima-i-rabt	كلمهٔربط	A copula, (Do.)
Kántá	कांटा	Proof, (Arithmetic).
Kasr-ul-Azlá'	كسرالاضلاع	A multilateral figure ; a polygon, (Euclid).
Kasr	كسر	(1) a fraction ; (2) the numerator of a fraction, (Arithmetic).
Kajautí	कटौती	A discount, (Do.)
Khabar	خبر	A predicate, (Grammar).
Khákná	خاكنه	An Isthmus, (Geography).
Khalíj	خليج	A bay or a gulf, (Do.)
Kháŗí	खाड़ी	A gulf, (Do.)
Khárij-i-Qismat	خارج قسمت	Quotient, (Arithmetic).

Vocabulary of Hindustání Technical Terms.—continued.

HINDUSTÁNÍ TECHNICAL TERMS USED IN ORDINARY VERNACULAR EDUCATIONAL BOOKS.		THEIR EQUIVALENTS OR MEANINGS IN ENGLISH.
Khatt	خط	A line, (Euclid).
Khatt-i-Istiwá............	خطِ استوا	The equator, (Geography).
Khatt-i-Jadí	خطِ جدی	The tropic of Capricorn, (Do.)
Khatt-i-Mumáss	خطِ مماس	A tangent, (Euclid).
Khatt-i-Mustaqím	خطِ مستقیم	A straight line, (Do.)
Khatt-i-Saratán	خطِ سرطان	The tropic of Cancer, (Geography).
Khitáb	خطاب	A title of honour, (Grammar).
Khushkí	خشکی	Land, (Geography).
Khusúf...................	خسوف	An eclipse of the moon, (Do.)
Khutút-i-Mustaqíma-i-Mutawáziya,	خطوطِ مستقیمہ متوازیہ	The parallel straight lines, (Euclid).
Khutút-i-Mutasáwiyat-ul-ab'ád....	خطوطِ متساویت الابعاد	Equi-distant straight lines, (Do.)
Khutút-i-Wahdání	خطوطِ وحدانی	Brackets or vinculum, (Algebra).
Koh-i-Átish-fishán	کوہِ آتش فشاں	A volcano, (Geography).
Kunyat	کنیت	A patronymic, (Grammar).
Kura	کرہ	A sphere; a globe, (Geography).
Kusúf	کسوف	An eclipse of the sun, (Do.)
Kusúr...................	کسور	Fractions, (Arithmetic).

Term	Arabic	Definition
Kusúr-i-´Ámm	حسورعام	Vulgar Fractions, (Arithmetic).
Kusúr-i-A'sháríya	حسوراعشاریه	Decimal Do. (Do.)
Kusúr-i-Gair-Mahdúd	حسورغیرمحدود	Circulating or Recurring Decimals, (Do.)
Kusúr-i-Gair-Mutanáhí	حسورغیرمتناهی	Ditto. Ditto.
Kusúr-i-Mudauwar	حسورمدور	Ditto. Ditto.
Kusúr-i-Mutawálí	حسورمتوالی	Ditto. Ditto.
Kusúr-i-Mutawátir	حسورمتواتر	Ditto. Ditto.
Kusúr-i-Mutawátir-i-Khális	حسورمتواترخالص	A pure circulator, (Do.)
Kusúr-i-Mutawátir-i-Makhlút	حسورمتواترمخلوط	A mixed circulator, (Do.)

L.

Term	Arabic	Definition
Laqab	لقب	A surname, (Grammar.)

M.

Term	Arabic	Definition
Má-ba'd	مابعد	A letter or a word that follows another, (Do.)
Madár-i-Arzí	مدارارضی	The ecliptic, (Geography).
Ma'dúd	معدود	A noun qualified by a Numeral Adjective, (Grammar).
Mafrúq	مفروق	A subtrahend, (Arithmetic).
Mafrúq-Minhu	مفروق منہ	A number from which any number has been subtracted, (Do.)
Mafrúz	مفروض	A thing supposed or given; (Euclid).
Maf'úl	مفعول	An objective case, (Grammar).
Maf'úl-bi-hí	مفعول بہ	The objective of a Transitive Verb, (Do).
Maf'úl-fíh	مفعول فیہ	An accusative of time or place, as *rát* in, *rát bhar parhá*, and *Madrisa* in, *touh Madrise meṇ haí*, (Do).

Vocabulary of Hindustání Technical Terms.—continued.

Hindustání Technical Terms used in ordinary Vernacular Educational books.		Their Equivalents or Meanings in English.
Maf'úl-i-Mutlaq	مفعول مطلق	An absolute objective. A cognate accusative, as *mdr* in, *ek sakht Már Márí* (Grammar).
Maf'úl-i-Má-Lam-Yusamma-Fá'iluhú	مفعولِ ما لم يسمّ فاعله	(An objective to a Verb whose agent is not expressed). The nominative to a Passive Verb, as *Zaid* in, *Zaid máregayá*, (Do.)
Maf'úl-la-Hú	مفعول له	The accusative which indicates the reason of an action, as *'ilm ke liye* in, *main 'ilm ke liye madrise játá húṇ*, (Do.)
Maf'úl-Minhu	مفعول منه	An objective expressing an instrument by which an action has been done, as *Talwár* in, *Talwár se márá*, (Do.)
Magrib	مغرب	The West, (Geography).
Mahdúd	محدود	Finite, as a line, (Euclid).
Mahsús-ul-Kasr	محسوس الكسر	An aliquot part of a number, (Arithmetic).
Maidán	ميدان	A plain, (Geography).
Mailán	ميلان	An inclination, (Euclid).
Majhúl	مجهول	Unknown, (Algebra).
Majmú's	مجموع	The sum of 2 or more quantities, (Euclid).
Majrúr	مجرور	An objective governed by a preposition, (Grammar).
Majzúr	مجذور	The square number, (Arithmetic).
Makhraj	مخرج	A denominator, (Do.)
Maksúr	مكسور	(1) a consonant marked with the vowel point *kasra* or *zer*, (Grammar). (2) a fraction, (Arithmetic).

Maksúr-i-Gair-Wájib	كسرغيرواجب	An improper fraction, (Arithmetic).
Maksúr-i-Mufrad	كسرمفرد	A simple fraction, (Do.)
Maksúr-i-Multaff	كسرملتف	A complex fraction, (Do.)
Maksúr-i-Murakkab	كسرمركب	A mixed fraction, (Do.)
Maksúr-i-Muzáf	كسرمضاف	A compound fraction, (Do.)
Maksúr-i-Wájib	كسرواجب	A proper fraction, (Do.)
Mál	مال	The square of a number, (Arithmetic and Algebra).
Mál-i-Ka'b	مال كعب	The fifth power of a number, (Do.)
Mál-ul-Mál	مال المال	The fourth power of a number, (Do.)
Ma'lúm	معلوم	Known, as a quantity, (Algebra).
Mamba-'i-Daryá	منبع دريا	The source of a river, (Geography).
Mandúb	مندوب	A noun governed by an interjection, (Grammar).
Manfí	منفى	(1) Negative, (Grammar). (2) Minus, (Algebra).
Manshúr	منشور	A prism.
Máp-tol	मापतोल	Measures and weights, (Arithmetic).
Má-qabl	ماقبل	An antecedent, (Grammar).
Maqádír	مقادير	Quantities, (Algebra).
Maqádír-i-Majhúla	مقادير مجهلة	Unknown quantities, (Do.)
Maqádír-i-Ma'lúma	مقادير معلومة	Known quantities, (Do.)
Maqádír-i-Manfíya	مقادير منفية	Negative Do. (Do.)

Vocabulary of *Hindustáni Technical Terms.*—continued.

HINDUSTÁNÍ TECHNICAL TERMS USED IN ORDINARY VERNACULAR EDUCATIONAL BOOKS.		THEIR EQUIVALENTS OR MEANINGS IN ENGLISH.
Maqádír-i-Mufrada	مقادیر مفرده	Simple quantities or monomials, (Algebra).
Maqádír-i-Mukhtalif-ul-Quwá	مقادیر مختلف القوی	Quantities of unlike powers or dimensions, (Do.)
Maqádír-i-Musbata	مقادیر مثبته	Positive quantities, (Do.)
Maqádír-i-Mutamásils	مقادیر متماثل	Like quantities, (Do.)
Maqála	مقاله	A book of Euclid.
Maqsúm	مقسوم	A dividend, (Arithmetic).
Maqsúm-'Alaih	مقسوم علیه	A divisor, (Do.)
Maqsúm-'Alaih-A'zam	مقسوم علیه اعظم	The greatest common measure, (Do.)
Maqsúm-'Alaih-Imtihání	مقسوم علیه امتحانی	A trial divisor, (Do.)
Maqsúm-'Alaih-Muwáfiq	مقسوم علیه موافق	An aliquot part of a number, (Do.)
Maqúla	مقوله	A saying, (Grammar).
Markaz	مرکز	A centre, (Euclid).
Marji-'i-Zamir	مرجع ضمیر	The substantive for which a pronoun stands, (Grammar).
Masala	مسئله	A theorem, (Euclid).
Masdar	مصدر	See *Ism-i-Masdar*.
Masdar-i-Gair-Waz'i	مصدر غیر وضعی	A counterfeit infinitive as نَ *z* (*badalná*) wherein the suffix *ná*, the Hindi sign of the infinitive, has been added to the Arabic word *badal*, (Grammar).

i-Wazl	A genuine Infinitive, (Grammar).
....	Exercise, (Arithmetic)
....	The East (Geography).
....	A Substantive followed by another in apposition, (Grammar)
....	Words or clauses connected together by a conjunction, (Grammar)
....	A noun qualified by an adjective, (Do.)
......a	A consonant marked with the vowel point *zamma*, (Do.)
....	A multiplicand, (Arithmetic),
......ffh	A multiplier, (Do.)
....	Time, (Do.)
...i-Zamin	The axis of the earth, (Geography).
...arnā	To subtract, (Arithmetic)
....	A zone, (Geography).
...-i-Bárida	A frigid zone, (Do.).
...t-ul-Buráj	The zodiac, (Do).
...-i-Hárra	The torrid zone, (Do.)
...-i-Mu'tadila	A temperate zone, (Do.)
....	A quantity, (Algebra).
...i-Mufrad	A simple Algebraical quantity,. (Do.)
...i-Murakkab	A compound (Do.)

Vocabulary of Hindustání Technical Terms.—continued.

HINDUSTÁNI TECHNICAL TERMS USED IN ORDINARY VERNACULAR EDUCATIONAL BOOKS.		THEIR EQUIVALENTS OR MEANINGS IN ENGLISH.
Mití-Káṭá	निमी कटा	Discount, (Arithmetic).
Mízán	میزان	(1) total, (2) proof, (Do.)
Mu'aiyan	معین	A rhombus, (Euclid).
Munkkad	مؤکد	A noun to which a word is added by way of confirmation, as *wuh* in the phrase *wuh khud*, (Grammar).
Mu'áwaza	معاوضه	Exchange, (Arithmetic).
Mu'áwin	معاون	The tributary of a river (Geography).
Mubaiyan	مبین	A word or a clause to which the succeeding clause serves as an explanation, as *yih* in the sentence, *main yih kahtá hún ki tum 'ilm tahsíl karo*, (Grammar).
Mubdal	مبدل	A word put in apposition, (Do.)
Mubdal-min-hu	مبدل منه	A noun to which some other noun has been put in apposition, (Do.)
Mubtadá	مبتدا	The subject of a sentence, (Grammar).
Mufazzal	مفضل	A noun qualified by an Adjective of the comparative degree, (Do.)
Mufazzal-'alaih	مفضل علیه	A noun with which another has been compared, as *Zaid* in *Zaid Bakr se hoshyár hai*, (Grammar).
Mufrad	مفرد	(1) simple, (2) single, (Algebra and Grammar).
Muhaddab-Hissa-i-muhít	محدب حصّه محیط	A convex circumference (Euclid).
Muhít	محیط	Circumference (Do.).

Muhual	كال	A word which means nothing (Grammar).
Mujauwaf-Hissa-i-muhit		A concave circumference, (Euclid).
Muku'ab		Cubic, (Arithmetic).
Mukhammas		A Pentagon, (Euclid).
Mukhátab		The person spoken to, or the 2nd person, (Grammar).
Malk		A country, (Geography).
Mumaiyaz		A word or a phrase the indistinctness of which is removed by the addition of a word called its tamiz, as das in das rupai, (Grammar).
Munádá		A Noun or a Pronoun in the Vocative case, (Grammar).
Munharif		A Trapezium, (Euclid).
Muntabiq honá		To coincide, (Do.)
Muqaddam		The antecedent terms in a Proportion (Algebra).
Muqaddar		A word understood though not expressed, (Grammar).
Muqsam bi-hi		That by which one swears, (Do.)
Murábba'		A square (Euclid).
Murakkab		Compound : a combination of words, (Grammar).
Murakkab-i-ġair-mufíd		An incomplete sentence, (Do.)
Murakkab-i-imtizáji		A combination of two nouns forming together the name of a thing, as mahzi-mandi, (Do.)
Murakkab-i-Isnádí		A complete sentence, (Do.)
Murakkab-i-Izáfi		A combination of noun in the Possessive case with one that governs it, (Do.)

HINDUSTÁNÍ TECHNICAL TERMS USED IN ORDINARY VERNACULAR EDUCATIONAL BOOKS.		THEIR EQUIVALENTS OR MEANINGS IN ENGLISH.
Murakkab-i-Mufid	....	⎱ A complete sentence, (Grammar).
Murakkab-i-Támm	....	⎰
Murakkab-i-Náqis	....	An incomplete sentence, (Do.)
Murakkab-i-Tausifí	....	A combination consisting of an adjective and the noun it qualifies, (Do.)
Murakkab-i-Ti'dádi	....	A compound numeral, as *ekattis* (31) *ek* and *tis* (Do.)
Mussabba'	....	A heptagon, (Euclid).
Musaddas	....	An hexagon, (Do.)
Musallas	....	A triangle, (Do.)
Musallas-i-Hádd-uz-Zawáyá	....	An acute-angled triangle, (Do.)
Musallas-i-mukhtalif-ul-azlá'	....	A scalene triangle, (Do.)
Musallas-i-munfarij-uz-záwiya	....	An obtuse-angled triangle, (Do.)
Musallas-i-mutasáwí-ul-azlá'	....	An equilateral triangle, (Do.)
Musallas-i-mutasáwí-us-sáqain	....	An isosceles triangle, (Do.)
Musallas-i-qáim-uz-záwiya	....	A right-angled triangle, (Do.)
Musamman	....	An octagon, (Do.)
Musáwát	....	An equation, (Algebra.)
Musáwát-i-dareja-i-awwal	....	A simple equation, (Do.)

Musáwát-i-darnja-i-duwum......	شاخ	A quadratic equation, (Do.)
Musáwát-i-darnja-i-duvvum-makhlút-ul-quwá		An adfected quadratic equation (Do.)
Musáwát-i-do-maqádir-i-majhúla ...		An equation of two unknown quantities, (Algebra).
Musáwát-i-sharti......		An equation of condition, (Do.)
Musáwát-i-záti		An identical equation, (Do.)
Musáwi		Equal, (Euclid).
Musbat......		1, Affirmation, (Grammar). 2, Positive ; plus (Algebra).
Mushabbah......		A thing compared to some other thing, (Grammar).
Mushabbah-bi-hi		The thing to which any thing is compared, (Do.)
Mushábih-i-fi'l		An adjective, a noun of agency or a Perfect Participle is a Mushábih-i-fi'l (quasi verb), (Grammar).
Mushár-ilaih		The noun to which a demonstrative adjective Pronoun refers, (Do.)
Musnad		A predicate (Do.)
Musnad-ilaih		The subject of a sentence, (Do.)
Mustasná......		Exception (Do.)
Mustasná-min-hu ...		That to which anything is an exception (Do.)
Mustatíl		An oblong, (Euclid).
Mutabáitile záwiye		Alternate angles (Do.)
Mutakallim		The speaker or the 1st person (Grammar).
Mutamásil		Like, (as quantities in Algebra).

Vocabulary of Hindustani Technical Terms.—continued.

TERMS USED IN ORDINARY VERNACULAR UCATIONAL BOOKS.	THEIR EQUIVALENTS OR MEANINGS IN ENGLISH.
مُتَمِّمَه	A complement, (Euclid).
مُتَناسِب	Proportional (Algebra).
مُتَساوِی الاَضلاع	Equilateral, (Euclid).
مُتَساوِی الاَضلاع و الزوایا	Equilateral and Equiangular, (Do.)
مُتَشابِہ	Similar (Do.)
مُتَوازی	Parallel, (Do.)
مُجتَمِع الاِشارات	Quantities having like signs, (Algebra).
مُضاف	The governing noun of a genitive (Grammar).
مُضاف الیہ	The genitive (Do.)
مُذَکَّر	Masculine, (Do.)
نَفع و نُقصان	Profit and loss, (Arithmetic).
نَفی	Minus, (Algebra).
نَحو	Syntax, (Grammar).
خاکِستان	An oasis, (Geography).
نَکِرہ	See *Ism-i-Nakira.*
نِسبَت	The denominator of a fraction, (Arithmetic).

Nazíra	نظیره	Homologous, (Euclid).
Nisbat	نسبت	Ratio, (Algebra).
Nisbat-i-kalán	نسبت کلان	A ratio of greater inequality, (Do.)
Nisbat-i-khurd	نسبت خورد	
Nisbat-i-kochak	نسبت کوچک	A ratio of less inequality, (Do.)
Nisbat-i-qillat	نسبت قلت	
Nisbat-i-musáwát	نسبت مساوات	A ratio of equality, (Do.)
Nisbat-i-mushtarik	نسبت مشترک	A common ratio, (Do.)
Nisbat-i-ziyáda	نسبت زیاده	A ratio of greater inequality, (Do.)
Nisf-Dáira	نصف دائره	Semi-circle, (Euclid).
Nisf-Kura-i-Zamín	نصف کره زمین	A Hemisphere, (Geography).
Nisf-un-Nahár	نصف النهار	Meridian, (Do.)
Niqát-i-Samt	نقاط سمت	The cardinal points of the compass, (Do.)
Nizám-i-Shamsí	نظام شمسی	The solar system, (Do.)
Nún-i-Gunna	نون غنّه	The letter nún when pronounced nasally, (Grammar).
Nuqta	نقطه	A point, (Euclid).
Nuqta-i-Tamáss	نقطه تماس	The point of contact, (Do.)
Nuqúsh-i-Jabriya	نقوش جبریه	Algebraical symbols, (Algebra).
Nuzúl	نزول	Evolution, (Do.)

Vocabulary of Hindustání Technical Terms.—continued.

Hindustání Technical Terms used in ordinary Vernacular Educational books.		Their Equivalents or Meanings in English.
P.		
Pachchham	पछम	The West, (Geography).
Pahár	पहाड़	A mountain, (Do.)
Pahárá	पहाड़ा	A multiplication table, (Arithmetic).
Paháṛi	पहाड़ी	A hill, (Geography).
Paimáyish	بیماییش	Measurement, surveying, (Arithmetic, &c.)
Paimáyish-i-Mujussamát-ká-andáza	بیماییش مجسمات کا اندازه	Solid or cubic measure, (Do.)
Paimáyish-i-Musattahát-ká-andáza	بیماییش مسطحات کا اندازه	Measures of surface, or the square measure, (Do.)
Puimáyish-i-Túlání-ká-andázn	بیماییش طولانی کا اندازه	Lineal measure, (Do.)
Púrab	पूरब	The East, (Geography).
Q.		
Qá'ida	قاعده	A base, (Euclid).
Qáim-uz-zawáyá	قائم الزوایا	A rectangle, (Do.)
Qánún-i-Musellasí	قانون مثلثی	The Rule of Three, (Arithmetic).
Qatár-i-Koh	قطار کوه	A range of hills or mountains, (Geography).
Qattá-'i-Dáíra	قطاع دائره	The sector of a circle, (Euclid).
Quus	قوس	An arc, (Do.)

Term	Arabic	Definition
Qaus-i-Quzaḥ	قوس قزح	The rainbow, (Geography).
Qímat-i-'Adadí	قيمت عددى	The numerical value, (Algebra).
Qímat-i-Naqd	قيمت نقد	The present worth, (Arithmetic).
Qiṭ'a-i-Dáira	قطعه دائره	The segment of a circle, (Euclid).
Qiṭ'át-i-Mutashábiha	قطعات متشابهه	Similar segments, (Do).
Qiyásí	قياسى	Regular, (Grammar).
Quṭb-i-Janúbí	قطب جنوبى	The South Pole, (Geography).
Quṭb-i-Shamálí	قطب شمالى	The North Pole, (Do.)
Quṭr	قطر	A diameter or a diagonal, (Euclid).
Quwá-i-Mutanázila	قواى متنازله	Descending powers, (Algebra).
Quwá-i-Mutasá'ida	قواى متصاعده	Ascending powers, (Do.)
Qúwat	قوت	The power of an Algebraical quantity, (Do.)
Qúwat-Numá	قوت نما	An exponent or index of the power, (Do.)

R.

Term	Arabic	Definition
Rabt	ربط	Construction, (Grammar).
Raqam	رقم	A number, a sum, (Arithmetic).
Raqam-i-Mafrúz	رقم مفروض	A given number, (Do.)
Raqam-i-Murakkab	رقم مركب	A compound quantity, (Algebra).
Raqam-i-Mutlaq	رقم مطلق	An absolute or abstract quantity, (Do.)
Raqba	رقبه	Area, (Geography).

Vocabulary of Hindustání Technical Terms.—continued.

HINDUSTÁNÍ TECHNICAL TERMS USED IN ORDINARY VERNACULAR EDUCATIONAL BOOKS.		THEIR EQUIVALENTS OR MEANINGS IN ENGLISH.
Rás	رأس	1, A cape (Do.) 2, A vertex, (Euclid).
Rás-i-Jadi	رأس الجدي	The winter solstice, (Geography).
Rás-i-Saratán	رأس السرطان	The summer solstice, (Do.).
Rás-ul-Mál	رأس المال	Stocks, (Arithmetic).
Rod-Bár	رودبار	A channel, (Geography).
Rub-'i-Dáira	ربع دائره	A quadrant, (Euclid).
Rukn	رکن	A term of an Algebraical expression, (Algebra).
S.		
Sahíh	صحيح	Whole, integral, (number), (Arithmetic).
Sáhil	ساحل	A sea coast, (Geography).
Sahrá	صحرا	A desert, (Do.).
Saikrá	सैकड़ा	The hundreds of (units), (Arithmetic).
Saiyára	سياره	A planet, (Geography).
Saiyárát-i-Andarúni	سيارات اندروني	The planets whose orbits lie within that of the earth. The inferior planets. (Do.)
Saiyárát-i-Berúni	سيارات بيروني	The planets whose orbits enclose that of the earth. The superior planets, (Do.)
Sál-i-Kabísa	سال کبيسه	A leap-year (Arithmetic).

Transliteration	Arabic	Definition
Saná'i	كاعى	Founded on usage. Irregular, (Grammar).
Samáuiyu-i-Mutanásiba	نسبت متناسيه	A Double Rule of Three of three proportions, (Arithmetic).
Sank	سمك	Thickness, (Euclid).
Samt-ur-Rás	سمت الراس	Zenith, (Geography).
Sániya	ثانيه	A minute, (Do.)
Sáq	ساق	One of the two equal sides of an Isosceles triangle, (Euclid).
Sarf	صرف	Etymology. Accidence, (Grammar).
Sar-i-Miqdár	سر مقدار	The co-efficient of a quantity, (Algebra).
Sarmáya	سرمايه	Capital or Stock, (Arithmetic).
Sath	سطح	Surface. Superficies. Rectangle, (Euclid and Geography).
Sath-i-Murtafa'	سطح مرتفع	A table-land, (Do.)
Sath-i-Mustawí	سطح مستوى	A plane superficies, (Euclid).
Sath-i-Mutawází-ul-Azlá'	سطح متوازى الاضلاع	A parallelogram, (Do.)
Sath-i-Zamín	سطح زمين	The surface of the earth, (Geography).
Ser-Hásil	سر حاصل	Fertile land, (Do.)
Shabíh-bil-Mu'aíyan	شبيه بالمعين	A rhomboid, (Euclid).
Shakl	شكل	A figure. A proposition, (Do.)
Shakl-i-Jabríya	شكل جبريه	An Algebraical formula, (Algebra).
Shakl-i-Mustaqímat-ul-khutút	شكل مستقيمات الخطوط	A rectilineal figure, (Euclid).
Shamál	شمال	The North, (Geography).

Vocabulary of Hindustání Technical Terms.—continued.

HINDUSTÁNÍ TECHNICAL TERMS USED IN ORDINARY VERNACULAR EDUCATIONAL BOOKS.		THEIR EQUIVALENTS OR MEANINGS IN ENGLISH.
Sharákat	شراکت	Fellowship. Partnership, (Arithmetic.)
Sharákat-i-Gair-Mutasáwí	شراکتِ غیرِ متساوی	Compound fellowship, (Do).
Sharákat-i-Mukhtalif	شراکتِ مختلف	Do. Do.
Sharákat-i-Mutasáwí	شراکتِ متساوی	Simple Fellowship, (Do.)
Sharh	شرح	Rate, (Do.)
Shart	شرط	See *Jumla-i-shart*, (Grammar).
Shart-i-Úlá	شرطِ اولیٰ	The first term of a proportion, or the antecedent of a ratio, (Arithmetic).
Shart-i-Ukhrá	شرطِ اخریٰ	The second term of a proportion, or the consequent of a ratio, (Do.)
Shisha-i-Musallasí	شیشۂ مثلثی	The prism.
Shumár-Kuninda	شمار کنندہ	The numerator of a fraction, (Arithmetic).
Sifat	صفت	An Adjective, (Grammar).
Sifat-i-Mushabbah	صفتِ مشبہ	A simple attributive Adjective, (Do.)
Sifat-i-Nisbatí	صفتِ نسبتی	A Relative Adjective as *Hindustání* (relating to Hindustán), (Do.)
Sifat-i-'Adadí	صفتِ عددی	A Numeral Adjective, (Do.)
Sifr	صفر	A cipher, (Arithmetic).
Síga	صیغہ	The conjugation or inflection of a Verb, (Grammar).
Sila	صلہ	The clause immediately following a Relative Pronoun, (Do.)

Silsila	سلسلة	A series, (Algebra).
Silsila-i-Jam'-o-Tafríq	سلسلۀ جمع و تفریق	Arithmetical progression, (Do.)
Silsila-i-Koh	سلسلۀ کوه	A mountain chain, (Geography).
Silsila-i-Músíqí	سلسلۀ موسیقی	Harmonical progression, (Algebra).
Silsila-i-Zarb-o-Taqsím	سلسلۀ ضرب و تقسیم	Geometrical progression, (Do.)
Sitta-i Mutanásiba	ستۀ متناسبه	The Double Rule of Three, (Arithmetic).
Subút	ثبوت	Proof, (Arithmetic &c.)
Súd	سود	Interest, (Do.)
Súd-dar-Súd	سود در سود	Compound Interest, (Do.)
Su'úl	سؤال	Involution, (Algebra).
Suwál	سوال	(1), Question, (Arithmetic and Algebra), 2, Problem, (Euclid).
T.		
Tábi'	تابع	Appositive, (Grammar).
Tábi-'i-Mugníyím	تابع مغنيم	The nouns of place and time, and the words *qadar, tarḥ,* and *waẓá'*, (Do.)
Tábi-'i-Muhmal	تابع مهمل	An unmeaning word joined to another, as *múṭ* in *jhúṭ múṭ*, (Do.)
Tafríq	تفریق	Subtraction, (Arithmetic).
Tafríq-i-Murakkab	تفریق مرکب	Compound subtraction, (Do.)
Tafẓíl-i-Ba'z	تفضیل بعض	An Adjective of the comparative degree, (Grammar).
Tafẓíl-i-Kull	تفضیل کل	The superlative degree of an Adjective, (Do.)
Tafẓíl-i-Nafsí	تفضیل نفسی	The positive or simple degree of an Adjective, (Do.)

Vocabulary of Hindustání Technical Terms.—continued.

HINDUSTÁNÍ TECHNICAL TERMS USED IN ORDINARY VERNACULAR EDUCATIONAL BOOKS.		THEIR EQUIVALENTS OR MEANINGS IN ENGLISH.
Taḥwíl		Conversion or reduction, (Arithmetic).
Takhallus		A poet's *nom de plume*, (Grammar).
Tákíd		A corroborative word, as (*khud*) in *wuh khud maujúd thá*, (Do).
Táli		The consequent term in a ratio, (Algebra).
Tamíz		A specificative Adverb, (Grammar).
Tamíz-i-Kammiyat		Distinction of number, (Do).
Tanásub		Proportion, (Algebra and Arithmetic).
Tanásub-i-Mufrad		A simple proportion. The Rule of Three, (Arithmetic and Algebra).
Tanásub-i-Murakkab		A compound proportion, the Double Rule of Three, (Do.)
Tánís		The feminine gender, (Grammar.)
Tankír		The indeterminateness (of a noun), (Do.)
Tansíf		Bisection, (Euclid.)
Táq		An odd number, (Arithmetic).
Taqátu'		Intersection, (Euclid).
Taqsím		Division, (Arithmetic).
Taqsím-i-Murakkab		Compound Division, (Do.)
Tarí		Water (in opposition to dry land), (Geography).

Ta'ríf	تعريف	1, The determinateness of a noun, (Grammar), 2, A definition.
Taríq-ueh-Shams	طريق الشمس	The zodiac. The Ecliptic, (Geography).
Tarkíb	تركيب	Parsing, (Grammar).
Taslís	تثليث	Trisection, (Euclid).
Tasríf	تصريف	Conjugation, declension, (Grammar).
Tawassut-i-Aqsát	توسط الاقساط	The equation of payment, (Arithmetic).
Tazkír	تذكير	The masculine gender, (Grammar).
Ti'dád-i-Marátib	تعداد مراتب	The number of terms or places, (Arithmetic).
Túl	طول	Length, (Do.)
Túl-i-Balad	طول بلد	The longitude, (Geography).

U.

Ufq, yé, Ufuq	افق	Horizon, (Geography).
'Ulúm-i-Muta 'árifs	علوم متعارفه	The axioms, (Euclid).
'Umq	عمق	Depth, (Arithmetic).
Uqlídis...............	اقليدس	Euclid.
'Urf...............	عرف	The name by which a person is generally known ; an alias, (Grammar).
Ustuwána	استوانه	A cylinder, (Euclid).
Usúli-Mauzú'a	اصول موضوعه	The Postulates, (Do).
Uttar	उत्तर	The North, (Geography).

Vocabulary of Hindustáni Technical Terms.—continued.

HINDUSTÁNÍ TECHNICAL TERMS USED IN ORDINARY VERNACULAR EDUCATIONAL BOOKS.		THEIR EQUIVALENTS OR MEANINGS IN ENGLISH.
W.		
Wafq-i-Mushtarik	وفق مشترک	A common factor, (Arithmetic.)
Wahdat	وحدت	The state of being singular in number, (Grammar.)
Wájid	واحد	Singular number, (Do.)
Wasat-fin-Nisbat	وسط في النسبت	A mean proportional, (Euclid).
Watar	وتر	The side of a triangle subtending an angle, (Do.)
Watar-i-Qáima	وتر قائمه	An Hypotenuse, (Do.)
Y.		
Yá-i-Majhúl	یائے مجهول	The letter ی (ye) when pronounced like e in 'there,' is called yái majhúl or the unknown 'ye,' (Grammar).
Yá-i-Ma'rúf	یائے معروف	The letter ی (ye) when pronounced like e in 'me,' is called yái ma'rúf or the known 'ye,' (Do.)
Z.		
Zamír	ضمير	See "Ism-i-zamír."
Zamír-i-Báriz	ضمير بارز	An expressed pronoun, (Grammar).
Zamír-i-Fá'il	ضمير فاعل	A personal pronoun of the nominative case, (Do.)
Zamír-i-Maf'úl	ضمير مفعول	A personal pronoun of the objective case, (Do.)
Zamír-i-Mustatar	ضمير مستتر	An implied pronoun (Do.)

Zamír-i-Muzáf-ilaih	ضمیر مضاف الیہ	A personal pronoun of the possessive case, (Do.)
Zarb	ضرب	Multiplication, (Arithmetic).
Zarb-i-Murakkab	ضرب مرکب	Compound multiplication, (Do.)
Zar-i-Asl	زر اصل	The principal (money), (Do.)
Zawát-ul-Aznáb	ذوات الاذناب	Comets, (Geography).
Zawáyá-i-Mutabádila	زوایائے متبادلہ	Alternate angles, (Euclid).
Do. Muttasila	زوایائے متصل	Adjacent angles, (Do.)
Zawi-l-'Uqúl	ذوی العقل	Rational beings, (Grammar).
Záwiya	زاویہ	An angle, (Euclid).
Záwiya-fil-Qit'a	زاویہ فی القطعہ	An angle in a segment, (Euclid).
Záwiya-i-Dákhila	زاویہ داخلہ	An interior angle, (Do.)
Záwiya-i-Hádda	زاویہ حادہ	An acute angle, (Do.)
Záwiya-i-Khárija	زاویہ خارجہ	An exterior angle, (Do.)
Záwiya-i-Markazí	زاویہ مرکزی	An angle at the centre of a circle, (Do.)
Záwiya-i-Muhít	زاویہ محیط	An angle at the circumference of a circle, (Do.)
Záwiyn-i-Munfarija	زاویہ منفرجہ	An obtuse angle, (Do.)
Záwiya-i-Musattaha	زاویہ مسطحہ	A plane angle, (Do.)
Záwiya-i-Musattahu-i-Mustaqímnat-ul-Khattain	زاویہ مسطحہ مستقیم الخطین	A plane rectilineal angle, (Do.)
Záwiya-i-Mustaqímat-ul-Khattain	زاویہ مستقیمات الخطین	A rectilineal angle, (Do.)
Záwiya-i-Qáima	زاویہ قائمہ	A right angle, (Do.)

Vocabulary of Hindustáni Technical Terms.—concluded.

HINDUSTÁNÍ TECHNICAL TERMS USED IN ORDINARY VERNACULAR EDUCATIONAL BOOKS.		THEIR EQUIVALENTS OR MEANINGS IN ENGLISH.
Zazaq	زَزَق	L. C. M. (least common multiple), (Arithmetic).
Zi'f	ضِعف	A multiple, (Do.)
Zila'	ضِلع	1. The side of a triangle (Euclid), 2, a district or country, (Geography).
Zú-Arba'at-il-Azlá'	ذُوالاَربَعَةِ الاَضلاع	A quadrilateral figure, (Euclid).
Zú-Az'áf	ذُوالاَضعاف	A common multiple, (Arithmetic).
Zú-Az'áf-i-Aqall	ذُوالاَضعافِ الاَقل	A Least Common Multiple, (Do).
Zul-hál	ذُوالحال	A Noun whose circumstance has been described by a word called *hál*, (Grammar).
Zú-Sulásat-il-Azlá'	ذُوالثُلاثَةِ الاَضلاع	A trilateral figure, (Euclid).

www.ingramcontent.com/pod-product-compliance
Lightning Source LLC
Chambersburg PA
CBHW021438090426
42739CB00009B/1540

9783744644785